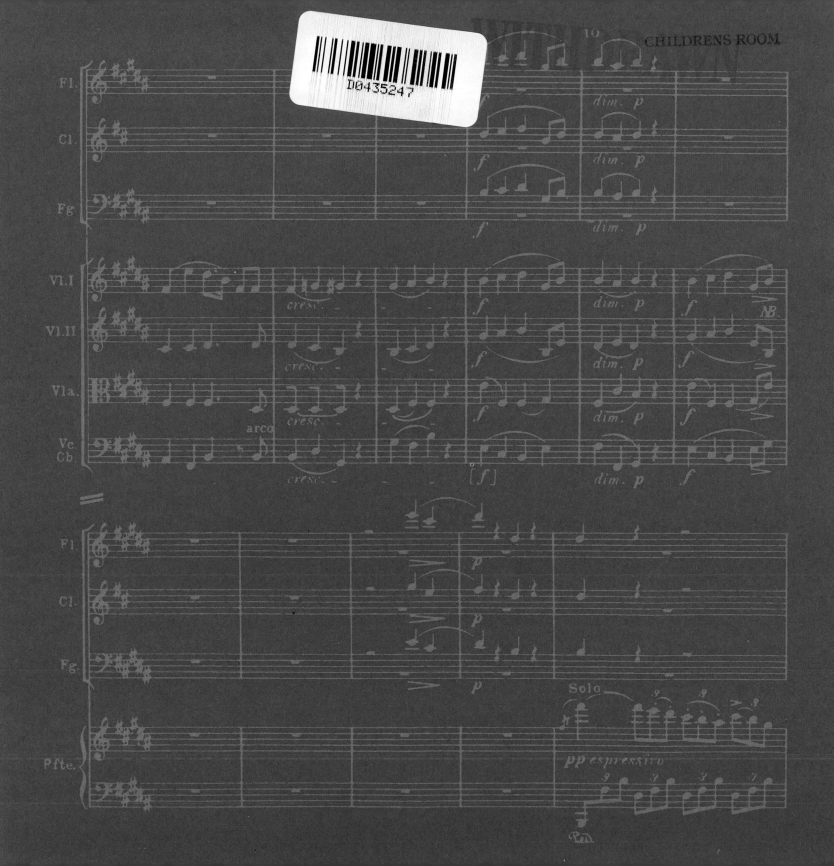

THE
COMPACT
VIOLIN

*A complete guide
to the violin and
ten great composers*

written by
Barrie Carson Turner

MACMILLAN

First published 1996 by Macmillan Children's Books
a division of Macmillan Publishers Limited
25 Eccleston Place, London SW1W 9NF
and Basingstoke

Associated companies throughout the world

ISBN 0 333 64030 6

9 8 7 6 5 4 3 2 1

A CIP catalogue record for this book is available from the British Library.

Typeset by Macmillan Children's Books
Colour Repro by Track QSP Ltd
Printed in Singapore

Text written by Barrie Carson Turner   **CHILDRENS ROOM**

Designer: Nigel Davies
Commissioning Editor: Susie Gibbs
Art Director: Anne Glenn
CD Consultant: Tony Locantro
Picture Researcher: Josine Meijer
Project Editor: Jane Robertson

Contents

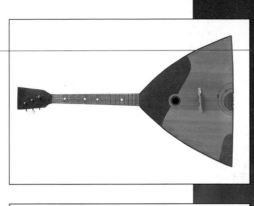

OVERTURE

Playing and listening to music, as well as learning about it, is one of the most popular and exciting pastimes in the world today.

The violin is equalled only by the piano in terms of the sheer volume of material written for it. It is one of the most versatile and popular members of the orchestra, able to mix with many different instruments. Bach, Beethoven, Mozart, Tchaikovsky, Vivaldi – the list of those who wrote great and important works for the violin include the most distinguished composers of the millennium.

Against a backdrop of changing attitudes to music, the violin developed from the early 'fiddle' which was an essential part of any folk gathering, into the sophisticated instrument that Antonio Stradivari eventually perfected in the early part of the eighteenth century.

The specially commissioned photographs on pages 18 and 19 show a modern violin maker, his workroom filled with half-made violins and maturing wood. These pictures show not only the enduring complexity of violin making, but also how very little has changed in the craft of hand-made stringed instruments since Stradivari's day.

The violin family is represented around the world by a range of different stringed instruments, from the balalaika in Russia to the Madagascan valiha. They are linked by the fact that they make music through the vibrations of a string or strings which are either plucked, as with the banjo, struck, as with the cimbalom, or bowed, as with the violin, the viola, the cello and the enormous double-bass.

The audio compact disc from EMI features extracts of music written by each of the ten great composers. The short section ON THE CD, which appears in the text for each composer, encourages a greater appreciation of the music being played.

Whether you are already a string player, just beginning lessons or simply interested in string playing, *The Compact Violin* will add to the range of your knowledge and understanding of the violin.

5

THE VIOLIN FAMILY

Violin

During the course of the violin's history several different designs have emerged. Two hundred years ago the small high-pitched violino piccolo was popular with composers. Around the same time a miniature elongated violin called a *kit* was played by dancing teachers to provide the music for lessons. But perhaps the most curious instrument of all was the Stroh violin. This violin, patented by Augustus Stroh in 1899 for use in early recording studios, had a large horn attached to it to amplify the sound.

Viola

The viola is very similar to the violin, although a little bigger in size, and longer by about six and a half centimetres. It is slightly deeper than the violin and has a richer tone. Many violinists also play the viola, as the fingering on both instruments is the same. An early relation of the viola, played over two hundred years ago, was the viola d'amore. 'Amore' means love and suggests the romantic sound of the instrument which was similar in size to the viola but had a decoratively shaped body and more strings. Extra strings underneath the playing strings vibrated of their own accord, enriching the tone of the instrument.

The viola has had much less music written for it than the violin, and throughout its history has known fewer solo performers. However, it forms an important section of the orchestra, and is an essential member of the string quartet.

The full name of the cello is violoncello, but today it is known simply as the cello. The cello is probably the most popular bass instrument in the orchestra, and has had some important music written for it, including chamber music and concertos.

Cello

The cello is much bigger than the violin and viola, with thicker strings, a stronger bow, and a broad, resonant body. Its tone is warm and mellow. At one time the instrument was held between the legs, but generally players now support the cello on a spike, which rests on the floor.

Two unusual cellos have been played in the past. The violoncello piccolo is a small cello sounding much higher than the ordinary cello. The arpeggione, a curious cross between a cello and a guitar, was invented by a Viennese instrument maker in 1823. Schubert heard and was attracted to this strange instrument, and later wrote his 'Arpeggione' sonata for it.

Double bass

Until a hundred years ago most double basses had only three strings, but now four strings is standard, in keeping with the rest of the violin family.

One of the biggest double basses was built by the French instrument maker Jean-Baptiste Vuillaume. His 'octo bass' stood a gigantic four metres high, and won him a medal at London's Great Exhibition of 1851. A series of levers pressed down the notes while the player bowed the instrument in the usual way – standing on a platform to do it!

STRING INSTRUMENTS AROUND THE WORLD

Banjo *(USA)*

The banjo originated in Africa, and was introduced into the USA in the days of the slave trade. Later it was taken up by colonial Americans, and by the early nineteenth century the instrument had reached Europe. The banjo was at one time popular with music hall performers and early jazz bands, but today it is less frequently heard.

Welsh Harp *(Wales)*

The national harp of Wales is called the *Telyn*. Early instruments were strung with horsehair, but later gut was substituted, which proved more serviceable and longer lasting. The early Welsh harp was later replaced by the *telyn deires*, the 'triple' harp, a bigger instrument with three rows of strings.

Guitar *(Spain)*

Today the guitar is played in almost every country in the world, although it originated in Spain where it is closely associated with traditional flamenco (gypsy) dancing. Many varying shapes and designs of the instrument are now available, and its electric counterpart is the foremost instrument of pop music.

Musical Bow

(East Coast, central South America)
The musical bow looks like a shooting bow, and is found in many parts of the world. The bow is held either vertically or horizontally and plucked with the fingers or a piece of bone called a plectrum, or sometimes bowed like a violin. Some bows have a gourd resonator attached to them to improve the sound, and others are played using the mouth as a resonator.

Kora

(West Africa, Gambia region)
The West African kora is both a harp and a lute. Players hold the instrument with the neck facing away from them and pluck the strings with the thumbs and forefingers of both hands. The large gourd resonator helps to improve and amplify the sound.

Balalaika *(Russia)*
The balalaika is one of Russia's most popular folk instruments. This unusually shaped instrument is made in six sizes for use in balalaika orchestras. It is also played singly, often accompanying a song or providing music for dancers.

Cimbalom *(Hungary)*
The metal strings of the Hungarian cimbalom (pronounced 'chimbalom') are struck with cloth-covered beaters, creating a pleasant buzzing sound. Also known as the dulcimer, it is popular in various forms throughout Eastern Europe. Today the cimbalom is often played by gypsy orchestras.

Pipa *(China)*
The pipa is one of the most popular string instruments of China. The instrument rests upright on the knees and is plucked by plectrums attached to each of the five fingers of the right hand. Music for the pipa is usually descriptive, representing natural sounds such as the wind blowing through reeds, or even fierce battles.

Koto *(Japan)*
The Japanese koto has thirteen silk strings and is 180 centimetres long. It is played with plectrums attached to the fingers of the right hand. At one time the koto was an important instrument of the royal court, but now it is played in the home, especially by women.

Valiha *(Madagascar)*
A thick stem of bamboo serves for the body of the Madagascan valiha. Slender strips of bamboo cut out of the stem but left attached at both ends of the instrument, serve as strings, while small blocks of wood raise the 'strings' away from the body of the instrument. The valiha is plucked with the finger nails.

Sitar *(India)*
The sitar is one of the most important instruments in India. The strings are plucked with a wire plectrum, attached to the right forefinger, while the fingers of the left hand pull the strings from side to side to create the well-known whining sound. It is said that to play the sitar well requires a lifetime of study.

Saùng *(Burma)*
The Saùng is the national instrument of Burma, and is one of the country's most beautiful instruments. The instrument is held diagonally across the player's body, resting on the knees, and it is plucked with the fingers.

INSTRUMENTAL GROUPS

Music for solo violin

Writing for an unaccompanied solo instrument is very difficult, but some composers, such as Bach and Ravel, have written successfully for solo violin, and many composers have written concertos for solo violin and orchestra.

Music for solo *unaccompanied* violin is unusual. This is probably because most people think a solo instrument sounds better against an accompaniment of different instruments; but also, an accompaniment allows a soloist to take an occasional few bars rest!

Duets

Duets are written for two performers. Although many duets are pieces in their own right, composers often write violin duets as learning material, with the second violin part intended to be played by the teacher. Violin sonatas were once considered to be solo pieces with accompaniment, but by Beethoven's time they had become true duets with both parts sharing the musical material equally.

Trios

A trio is for three performers. String trios are usually for violin, viola and cello. In Corelli's time, three hundred years ago, most composers wrote 'trio sonatas'. In fact these compositions (most often for two violins with equally important parts) were really duets with accompaniment. 'Piano trios', such as Beethoven's famous 'Archduke' Trio, are usually for piano with violin and cello, with all instruments assuming identical musical roles.

10

String quartets

The string quartet is probably the most popular chamber music combination of all time. (Chamber music is music for a small number of instrumentalists, suitable for intimate performances.) Haydn and Mozart wrote some of their most beautiful music for string quartets. To begin with, composers gave the first violins the most interesting music, but by the end of the eighteenth century it was usual to share the musical material uniformly among the players. However, the quartet leader has always remained the first violin.

Larger string groups

In 1825 the sixteen-year-old Mendelssohn wrote an octet for strings which has remained in the concert repertoire for over one hundred and fifty years. In 1827 Schubert wrote his much admired quintet for strings – for two violins, viola and two cellos. The sounds of assorted string instruments blend well together and work in virtually any combination. Tchaikovsky, in his 'Serenade for Strings', writes for an orchestra consisting entirely of strings.

The violin in the orchestra

String instruments have formed the backbone of the orchestra for almost four centuries. In the modern orchestra there are more violins (about thirty) than any other instrument, taking up about two thirds of the total players. The violins are divided into two groups – 'firsts' and 'seconds'. The leader of the first violins, who sits at the front near the conductor, is also the leader of the entire orchestra.

Orchestra

The first violins sit at the front of the orchestra, on the left of the conductor, with the second violins behind them. Each two violinists share a 'desk' or music stand. The player on the left (facing the conductor) is usually responsible for turning the pages of the music.

THE HISTORY OF THE VIOLIN

No one knows who made the first violin, almost five hundred years ago, but we do know that the violin is probably of Italian origin.

In the Middle Ages there were many different stringed instruments. Some were plucked, like the lute, and others were played with the bow. Two important stringed instruments contributing to the development of the violin are the rebec, a small pear-shaped fiddle, and a rather more elegant instrument called the lira da braccio. The first real violins had three strings and were often also referred to as rebecs until the word 'vyollon' came into use.

As the violin grew in popularity, specialist violin makers began to appear. The Italian town of Cremona led the way, and here the first of the great violin makers, Andrea Amati, set up his workshop. For three generations the Amati family restyled and improved the violin, resulting in a design virtually unaltered to this day.

A woman playing a rebec. This tapestry, dated 1550, is from the Fountain Workshop of the Loire. Note the pear-like shape of the instrument, and how it echoes the woman's figure.

The changing styles of the bow. These bows are dated (from top to bottom) 1620, 1640, 1660, 1700 and 1790.

Antonius Stradivarius Cremonenſis
Faciebat Anno 1732
de Annigy

Antonius Stradivarius Cremonenſis
Faciebat Anno 1737
D. Anni 93

More powerful instruments

Violin makers wanted not only to make violins that *looked* beautiful, but to make instruments that *sounded* beautiful. It was important, too, that the tone of an instrument should be powerful enough to carry well. Thus the bridge of the violin was heightened, and the finger board lengthened. Now the strings could be longer and tighter – resulting in a more robust tone.

Amati violins are still played today, but neither their elegance nor tone quality can match the instruments built by another Italian, who began his career as an apprentice in the Amati workshops – Antonio Stradivari.

Antonio Stradivari 1644–1737

Stradivari made the violin longer, strengthened the bodywork, and broadened the soundholes, thereby enriching the tone. He refined each small feature to give every violin that left his workshops a distinction revered throughout Europe.

Today, Strads are played by some of the world's finest violinists. They often have the same names as their previous owners – such as the 'Sarasate', named after the famous Spanish violinist.

By the beginning of the nineteenth century public concerts were well established and growing increasingly popular. Large concert halls were built where fashionable society met to enjoy music.

Better violin strings

The earliest violin strings were made of individual strands of sheep-gut twisted together. But although this was satisfactory for the two highest strings, gut produced a very inferior sound when used for the lower (slacker) strings. After 1690 a new technique was discovered, which involved binding an ordinary gut string with very fine wire. This produced a thicker string, with a much more reliable sound.

Above: The Merry Cottagers *by Thomas Sword. The violin occupies an important place in folk music. In many parts of the world village merrymaking and dancing is incomplete without one or more 'fiddlers'.*

Right: Paris, 1770. Paris and Milan were the two great centres of violin 'modernization'. Very few old violins of the early eighteenth century escaped rebuilding.

More difficult music

By the end of the eighteenth century, when composers like Mozart and Haydn were writing their most accomplished string works, a new generation of violinists capable of performing the new difficult music that composers were writing began to appear. However, this virtuoso style of playing demanded further improvements to the violin: it now had to be made sturdier, to bear the extra wear and tear.

As a virtuoso violinist, Spohr was immensely successful, and toured throughout Germany.

Rather than buying new instruments, performers wanted their old violins modernized, resulting in a new school of skilled instrument makers who specialized in the rebuilding of older instruments. Many changes were made. The woodwork of the belly and back of the instrument was shaved thinner to improve the tone, and the fingerboard was lengthened further to enable violinists to play much higher notes. At last the violin could face the powerful challenges – from both composer and concert hall – of the nineteenth century.

Tourte's improved bow

By the end of the eighteenth century the bow had reached its final form, with the French bowmaker, François Tourte (1747–1835). His new bow was more accurately balanced, more elastic and longer (enabling the violinist to play more notes in one bow strokc). Thc 'springiness' allowed the performer increased playing agility. Many nineteenth-century violin compositions would be very difficult to play using an old-style bow.

As the nineteenth century progressed, minor additions and improvements were made to the violin, bringing it in line with the instrument we know today. In 1819 the German violinist and composer, Louis Spohr, introduced a chin rest. This enabled the violin to be held more reliably on the shoulder, especially now that the left hand was changing position on the fingerboard more frequently. And finally, with the introduction of higher tension strings, 'adjusters' were fitted to the tailpiece, allowing an easier and more accurate alternative to tuning with the pegs.

François Tourte was known as the 'Stradivari of the bow'.

HOW THE VIOLIN WORKS

Instruments like the violin rely on vibrating strings to make their sound. The strings vibrate when the bow is drawn across them, but produce very little sound themselves. It is only when the vibrations are passed through the bridge to the large hollow body, or *soundbox* of the instrument that the tone grows powerful enough to be heard.

The sound holes help the vibrations generated in the body of the instrument to reach the open air, and eventually our ears, where they are converted into sound.

Bridge
Small grooves in the bridge keep the strings in place. Thinner strings have small plastic or rubber protectors to stop them cutting into the wood.

Tailpiece
Each string is fastened securely to the tailpiece or to an adjuster on the tailpiece.

Chin rest
The chin rest helps the player to grip the violin, and protects that part of the belly from wear.

Adjuster
A small tuning screw which enables the strings to be tuned very finely.

Sound holes
Sometimes called 'f' holes because of their shape.

Nut
Small grooves cut into this small raised piece of wood guide the strings along the fingerboard.

Scroll

Pegbox

Neck

Fingerboard
By pressing the strings against the fingerboard in different places, the violinist is able to play a wide range of notes stretching over three octaves.

Belly

Tuning pegs
The violinist tunes the instrument by twisting the tuning pegs backwards and forwards to tighten or slacken the strings. Violins go out of tune very easily, especially with changes of temperature, or on long journeys. A violinist must expect to tune a new instrument many times before the new strings 'settle in'.

Strings
The violin has four strings, all the same length but of different thicknesses. The thinner the string, the higher it sounds. The four strings of the violin (starting with the highest) are E, A, D and G.

Bow
The modern violin bow is made from many strands of horse hair fitted into each end of a long curving piece of wood. The hair is tightened for playing, and slackened when the bow is not in use. Slackening the bow helps preserve the springiness of the wood.

Screw

Sound post
One of the most important parts of the violin, this pencil-like wooden rod wedged between the back and front panels of the instrument improves the transfer of vibrations between the bridge and the soundbox.

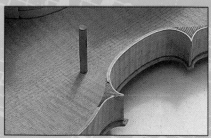

Soundwave of a violin

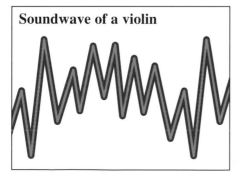

HOW THE VIOLIN IS MADE

More than seventy separate parts are needed to construct a new violin. Various different woods are used, which are deliberately chosen for their sound-carrying capabilities as well as for their strength. Spruce is chosen for the belly because it is soft and responds well to the vibrations of the strings, whereas the back of the instrument is made from maple, a much harder wood, which helps the violin to stand up to the wear and tear of its playing life. Many parts of violin-making are difficult and require careful judgement. The finest instruments are still made by hand, and great care is taken to ensure the beauty of the finished product.

The two pieces of spruce that make up the *belly* are cut very carefully to make certain that the grain matches up when they are glued together.

Two pieces of maple wood are shaped and glued together to make the *back* of the instrument.

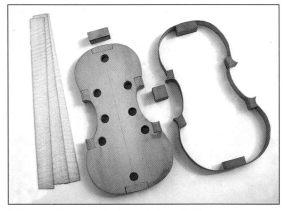

The maple wood *ribs* of the violin are moulded into shape on a template, using heat. Small blocks are fixed in the corners, and inside the top and bottom of the body to strengthen the construction.

The back is glued in position, and the '*f*' *holes* are carefully cut out of the belly using a template.

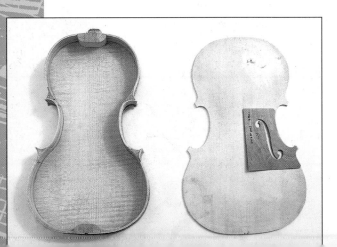

Narrow strips of pear, and white poplar wood, called *purfling,* are inlaid decoratively around the edge of the back and belly. The inlay helps guard against the wood panels splitting.

18

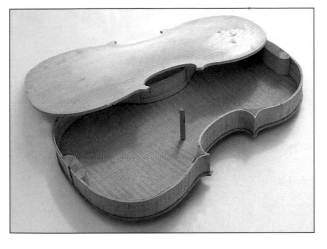

The pine *soundpost* is wedged tightly between the belly and the back of the instrument, near the treble foot of the bridge.

The violin maker's desk.

The *neck*, with its decorative *scroll*, is carved from maple wood.

Varnish not only contributes to the beauty of the violin but also protects the wood. Each new instrument is given many coats of varnish.

Except for the use of modern equipment, violin workshops have changed very little since Stradivari's day.

Making a violin is a highly skilled art which involves much delicate and detailed work.

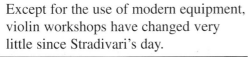

HOW THE VIOLIN IS PLAYED

We have already said that there are more violins in an orchestra than any other instrument. The string section of the orchestra plays more than the other sections, and most listeners to music say they can listen for much longer periods to string music than any other. Why is this so? The fact is, the violin is an amazingly versatile instrument. It sounds good massed together, it mixes well with other instruments, and there are many different ways of playing it. It's not surprising therefore that composers, performers and listeners alike are atttracted to it.

Pizzicato
Violinists don't always use the bow when they play – occasionally they pluck the strings. The word for this is pizzicato (pronounced 'pitzy-carto'). Violinists seldom play entire melodies pizzicato, as the sound doesn't carry very well, but in the ballet *Sylvia* the French composer Delibes has written an entire movement in which all the strings lay down their bows to play the famous 'Pizzicato Polka'. The word arco ('with the bow') cancels pizzicato, and players then revert to using the bow.

20

Playing with a mute

Fixing a wooden clamp over the bridge of the violin reduces the strength of the vibrations reaching the soundbox. This has the effect of muting, or damping the sound. Muted violins sound very gentle and distant. Composers use the Italian terms con sordini ('with mutes') and senza sordini ('without mutes').

Sul ponticello

Translated this means 'on the little bridge'. In violin music it tells the player to bow the strings close to the bridge. This creates a very thin, scratchy effect.

Col legno

The exciting beginning of 'Mars, the Bringer of War' from Holst's suite *The Planets* features the strings playing with a curious clicking sound. This is col legno – 'with the bow'. The bow is held on its side so that as each note is played the wood of the stick taps the string.

Vibrato

One of the most important string techniques. The left-hand finger holding down the note is 'rocked' slightly, causing a fluctuation in pitch, and enriching the tone. Vibrato is particularly effective on long notes. Some violinists prefer not to use vibrato when playing very old music.

Double stopping

Pressing a finger on to the fingerboard is called 'stopping' a note. 'Double stopping' means playing two notes at once. Some composers also write 'triple stopping' and even 'quadruple stopping' (three and four notes), but on the violin it is not really possible to play more than two notes at exactly the same time.

Playing harmonics

Harmonics are soft flute-like notes produced by touching a string very lightly (not pressing the note down) and drawing the bow across very gently. They are usually only used in fairly modern music.

Glissando

This word (which means 'sliding') directs the violinist to slide the finger from one note to another (which allows all the intervening sounds to be heard). Glissandos are rare outside twentieth-century music.

Bowing

Holding the bow properly is very important to good violin playing. The right hand controls the pressure of the bow hair on the strings, which affects the tone of the instrument. The player must also have a relaxed wrist.

VIVALDI

1678–1741

Almost all of Antonio Vivaldi's compositions involve the violin in some way. He wrote more than five hundred and fifty concertos, over half of which are for violin.

Vivaldi was introduced to the violin by his father Giovanni, himself a professional violinist who played in the famous cathedral orchestra of St Mark's in Venice. The young Antonio also studied the violin with Giovanni Legrenzi, choirmaster at St Mark's, and one of Venice's most highly respected composers and teachers.

By the time Antonio was in his teens, he was already playing the instrument professionally alongside his father. But even though it was clear that Antonio had a natural gift for music, Giovanni was determined that his son should dedicate himself to the church.

In 1703 Vivaldi was ordained as a priest, but decided not to pursue a church career. He accepted his first professional teaching appointment – as *maestro di violino* (violin professor) at the Ospedale della Pietà, a school dedicated to the care and upbringing of orphaned girls. The school was also a music academy, and here Vivaldi remained, teaching and playing, for most of his life. He became Concert Master and later Director of the school.

At the time of his appointment as violin professor, Vivaldi was writing his first string works: a set of trio sonatas (pieces with several movements, usually written for two violins and cello). Shortly after completing these works, Vivaldi wrote his first violin sonatas.

As his fame spread through Europe

The Venice of Vivaldi's day was a thriving city where the cultural life was rich and varied. It is not surprising that Vivaldi had no wish to make a permanent home elsewhere.

Right: Vivaldi's house. Although he enjoyed travelling, and several times accepted posts abroad, Vivaldi was never away from Venice for long.

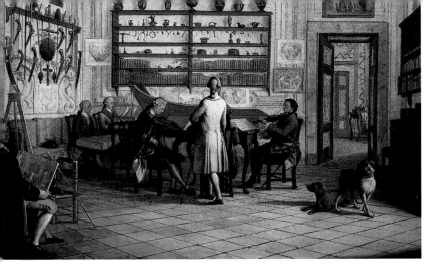

Two violins and a harpsichord play a trio sonata. A cello reinforces the bass line.

The composer wrote his most famous work for violin, *The Four Seasons*, in 1725. These four concertos – 'Spring', 'Summer', 'Autumn', and 'Winter' – describe in music the sights, sounds and pleasures of the changing seasons. Each concerto begins with a short poem, probably written by Vivaldi himself, and each line of the poetry has its own section of music.

*Spring is here, and gladly
The birds greet it with merry tune.
The streams, wafted by soft winds,
Gently whispering, begin their flow.*

Vivaldi received many commissions to compose works. He was greatly admired by other composers who often took inspiration from him for their own compositions. Bach was so impressed with Vivaldi's music that he transcribed five of the composer's violin concertos for keyboard – as a musical exercise, and for his own use.

L'ESTRO ARMONICO
CONCERTI
Consacrati
ALL' ALTEZZA REALE
DI
FERDINANDO III
GRAN PRENCIPE DI TOSCANA
Da D. Antonio Vivaldi
Musico di Violino e Maestro de' Concerti del
Pio Ospedale della Pietà di Venezia
OPERA TERZA
LIBRO PRIMO.

A AMSTERDAM
Aux depens D'ESTIENNE ROGER Marchand Libraire

In this picture the artist Sebastiano Mazzolini represents the season of spring with a painting of a young woman with flowers.

In 1711 Vivaldi published a set of twelve violin concertos which he called L'estro armonico. *The Italian words could be translated as 'harmonic inspiration', although the word* estro *actually means 'heat', suggesting Vivaldi composed these works in a 'fire of inspiration'!*

J. S. BACH

1685–1750

It was during Johann Sebastian Bach's lifetime that many of the features of the modern orchestra developed – such as the division of the violins into 'firsts' and 'seconds'. The violin's popularity as a solo instrument was enhanced by the fine instruments being produced by the new schools of Italian violin making.

The house where Bach was born, the youngest of eight children. The Bach family were far from wealthy and were beset with tragedy. When Johann was eight his mother died, and within a year his father too was dead.

The town of Eisenach where Bach lived as a boy. Bach was one of the most untravelled of all composers and was content to spend his entire life in northern Germany.

It is likely that Bach had his first violin tuition and music theory lessons from his father, a town musician in Eisenach, northern Germany. The young Bach progressed rapidly with his music studies and was soon an accomplished violinist.

When he was eighteen, Bach took a job as a violinist in nearby Weimar. After this, he began to compose music and never again had to rely on his violin playing as a source of income.

During the early part of his life Bach's composing skills were directed towards organ and choral music. It was not until he became chief Court Musician (he was called *Kapellmeister*) for Prince Leopold at Anhalt-Cöthen, composing for his own small orchestra, that he began to write his first instrumental music. This included two concertos for violin and orchestra that remain favourites with soloists all over

St Thomas's School, Leipzig, where Bach spent the last twenty-eight years of his life. He taught Latin as well as music to the choirboys of the school, and composed music for the church.

Right: *Bach's original manuscript for the opening of the Chaconne. This extremely difficult piece requires the violinist to play chords of two, three and even four notes.*

the world. Bach made the solo part in these concertos much more important than before, using the orchestra mostly as an accompaniment.

While working for Prince Leopold, Bach wrote three 'partitas' for violin. Partita No. 2 contains one of the most well-known pieces of music Bach wrote – the famous 'Chaconne'. This movement is so popular that it is often played at concerts as a single item. The piece begins with a powerful melody, which is followed by thirty-one variations.

During the same productive period Bach also wrote three violin sonatas. Both these and the Partitas are unusual in that they are for unaccompanied violin.

In about 1719 Bach met the Margrave of Brandenburg, an important member of the nobility and keen amateur musician who enjoyed commissioning concertos from composers whom he admired, like Bach. The result of their meeting was the famous Brandenburg Concertos.

During Bach's lifetime much of the glorious music he wrote was never appreciated. When the great composer died, ailing and blind, he was buried in an unmarked grave, and many of his most precious manuscripts were sold for only a few pence each.

ON THE CD
Partita No. 2 in D minor
BWV1004
I. Allemande II. Courante IV. Gigue

A gigue is a lively dance in three time, originally from England. It was usually the closing movement in a set of dances, but perhaps Bach places a gigue as the 4th movement in this piece because of the slow weighty 'Chaconne' that follows. Other movements in this partita are 'Allemande', a moderately slow dance from Germany; 'Courante', a fast dance from France; and 'Sarabande', a slow, stately Spanish dance. This is certainly a work with an international flavour!

TARTINI

1692–1770

Giuseppe Tartini wrote over four hundred works, and contributed many new ideas and techniques to the art of violin playing. Unfortunately, most of his compositional output remained unpublished during his lifetime.

Right: *One night in 1713 Tartini tells us he had a dream in which he saw and heard the devil playing the most wonderful music. As soon as the composer awoke he wrote down as much of the music as he could remember. Tartini called his piece 'The Devil's Trill' sonata because of the many trills in the last movement.*

Tartini was born into a well-to-do Italian family. From an early age it was clear that he was very musical. But plans were made for him to enter the church, then the law, and finally the army. None of these professions attracted him, but in 1709 he agreed to enter the university of Padua, although he knew this would restrict his development as a violinist and composer.

Three years later, he secretly married one of his pupils – but when the event was discovered, his new wife's guardian ordered the young student's arrest and Tartini was forced to flee Padua and go into hiding! However, at last released from a course of study he had no interest in, Tartini could now follow his chosen career.

The composer took lodgings in the monastery at Assisi and found a job as an orchestral violinist. Soon Tartini's reputation as a violinist and teacher began to grow, and at last, in 1721, it was safe to return to Padua where he became orchestral director and principal violinist at the Church of St Anthony.

ON THE CD
Sonata in A minor
V. Allegro assai –
Variations 1 to 6

The Sonata in A minor is a work for violin, viola da gamba, and harpsichord. The viola da gamba was a large string instrument very popular in Tartini's day, and the forerunner of our modern double bass.

In 1728 Tartini founded his own school of violin playing, which soon became acclaimed throughout Europe. Many of his students later became violinists and composers in their own right, such as the German composer, Johann Graun, and the violinist and composer, Pietro Nardini.

Tartini was not only interested in violin playing, but many other aspects of music as well. He made a study of acoustics, and discovered that when two notes are played together on the violin they create a third note. He called this third note the 'combination tone', and showed how it could help in tuning the violin. Today, violinists always tune the violin by playing two strings at a time. Listening for the correct combination tone makes tuning the violin easier.

Tartini wrote several books on violin playing and music theory. One of his most famous is *L'Arte dell'arco*, which is a detailed instruction book of violin bowing.

Tartini's signature. His spiky but flowing style suggests that he was a man of determination and character. In Tartini's day very few people other than scholars, artists and churchmen could read and write.

PIETRO NARDINI

The Italian violinist and composer Pietro Nardini (1722–1793) who was a pupil of Tartini.

HAYDN
1732–1809

At sixteen, Haydn left his schoolboy position as chorister at St Stephen's cathedral in Vienna and set out to earn his living as a keyboard and violin player, and as a teacher.

It was during these early years as a freelance musician that Haydn began writing his first string quartets (music for two violins, viola and cello). Through his pupils, Haydn had met Baron von Fürnberg, who commissioned the composer to write a set of string quartets. After he had completed this commission Haydn wrote

Franz Joseph Haydn's first harpsichord, violin and theory lessons were given to him by a cousin, Johann Matthias Frankh, a professional musician and teacher. Haydn made rapid progress – so much so that within two years he was accepted as a pupil at Vienna's celebrated St Stephen's choir school.

Rohrau in Austria where Haydn, the second of twelve children, was born on 31 March 1732. Making music and singing was a regular pastime in the Haydn household, and it is probably through such domestic music-making that Haydn developed his own love of folk music.

St Stephen's cathedral in Vienna where Haydn was a chorister for almost ten years.

Baron von Fürnberg's country house at Weinzierl where Haydn was engaged as a violinist.

further string quartets until, by the end of his life, he had written over eighty. Because he played a significant role in developing this musical form, Haydn is often known as 'the father of the string quartet'.

For most of his life Haydn worked for the wealthy Hungarian Esterházy family in their splendid new palace. Here he had the exciting job of being responsible for the entire musical output of the establishment. He wrote many new instrumental works for the Esterházy orchestra, including three violin concertos, which he may have performed himself, and over fifty string trios.

In his final few quiet years (he lived more or less in retirement from 1801) it probably never occurred to Haydn that international music society considered him the world's greatest living composer. Over his long life his fame had spread far and wide. In 1809 when Vienna was overrun with Napoleon's armies, a French guard was posted at his house to ensure his safety and, when he died, memorial services were held in every major city in Europe.

ON THE CD
String Quartet in D
('The Lark') Op. 64 No.5

Haydn wrote his six string quartets, Op. 64, in 1790, shortly before his first trip to London. 'The Lark' quartet is named after the soaring violin melody of the first movement. The music for this final movement is marked vivace, which means vigorous and energetic.

Haydn's employer, Prince Paul Anton Esterházy, was a passionate lover of music, the arts, and all things extravagant. His employees wore splendid uniforms, including even Haydn, seen here in his official livery.

MOZART

1756–1791

As a child of only three and a half Wolfgang Amadeus Mozart spent hours sitting at the keyboard exploring its various sounds. At four he could already play the harpsichord; and by five he was composing his own music, which his father wrote down for him.

Right: Both Mozart children were exceptionally gifted, but at concerts and functions it was always the younger Wolfgang who 'stole the show'. This picture of Leopold, Wolfgang and his sister Nannerl was painted in 1780 by Louis Carrogis de Carmontelle.

Mozart was eight years old when his first sonatas for the violin were published. He was born into a household in which the violin was very important. His father, Leopold, was a professional violinist, a violin teacher and a musician of international standing. He taught Wolfgang himself. But soon Leopold realized that his young son was not only interested in playing music – he also wanted to write it.

Mozart introduced many new ideas to the composing style he had inherited from Leopold. One important change he made to the violin sonata was to treat the violin and the piano as equals. The piano was now as important as the violin, and given its own interesting music to play.

When Mozart was nineteen, the Archbishop of Salzburg employed him to play the violin in the orchestra and to compose for the court. Mozart enjoyed both these duties, but the Archbishop treated him like an unskilled servant. It was not a happy situation. Yet Mozart continued to compose, now devoting himself to the violin. Within a year he had written five violin concertos for his own performance at court concerts. Even when unhappy and frustrated he could produce beautiful music.

Mozart died very young – at the age of thirty-five. It is truly amazing that he should have written so much music in so short a time.

At fourteen Mozart wrote his first string quartet – completed in a single evening. String quartets have been popular since the time of Haydn and Mozart.

SEI
QUARTETTI
PER DUE VIOLINI, VIOLA, E VIOLONCELLO
Composti e Dedicati
al Signor
GIUSEPPE HAYDN
Maestro di Cappella di S.A.
il Principe d'Esterhazy & &
Dal Suo Amico
W.A. MOZART
Opera X.
In Vienna presso Artaria Comp.
Mercanti d'Editori di Stampa Musica
e Carte Geografiche

Towards the end of his life Mozart's health, although never good, was made worse by financial worry. It is possible that the composer died from some inherited disorder, but even today no one knows the real cause of his death.

When Haydn heard Mozart's string quartets he shook his head in disbelief – he couldn't believe the amazing music he was hearing. He said to Leopold, 'your son is the greatest composer I know'.

Mozart at the age of six in the handsome clothes given to him by the Empress Maria Theresa. When the Empress, who was herself a reasonably gifted musician, heard of the talented Mozart children she invited them to her palace of Schönbrunn to play for her.

ON THE CD
Serenade in G
('Eine kleine Nachtmusik')
K525
I. Allegro

This is one of Mozart's most well-known works for strings. It was composed in 1787. On the recording you will hear the bright, energetic music of the first movement, in which the violins take the lead.

BEETHOVEN
1770–1827

Ludwig van Beethoven suffered dreadful hardship and poverty during his early life. His father managed to hold down a job as a minor musician, while teaching his son violin and piano. Ludwig, though only five, made rapid progress and by the age of seven played in his first public concert.

Right: *The beginning of the violin part of Beethoven's 'Kreutzer' sonata with much 'double stopping' (playing on several strings at once) in evidence. Although considered difficult in its day, the work is straightforward by today's standards.*

When he was eleven, Beethoven began studies with the Court Organist, Christian Gottlob Neefe, while continuing his violin and viola lessons. Beethoven began writing for violin and strings from an early age: by 1800, when he was only thirty, he had written a string quintet, several string trios, and twelve violin sonatas.

Composers of the day often treated the violin as inferior to the piano when the two instruments played together, but in his later works Beethoven always treats the two instruments as equals, and gives them both important music to play.

Beethoven dedicated one of his most famous violin sonatas to the French violinist, Rodolphe Kreutzer, whose playing he admired. Unfortunately Beethoven hadn't obtained permission for the dedication. When Kreutzer looked at the music he refused to perform it, saying that the work was 'outrageously unintelligible'!

It was true that Beethoven was writing music which was increasingly difficult. At a rehearsal for one of the composer's 'Razumovsky' string quartets, one of the violinists

complained that his part was too difficult. Beethoven was furious, and said, 'Does he really suppose that I think of his miserable little fiddle when the spirit speaks to me and I compose something?'

In 1802 Beethoven was told that the deafness he had experienced for some time was incurable. For a musician and composer no news could be worse. Yet shortly afterwards he wrote two of his most beautiful works – the Romances for violin and orchestra. In both these pieces the violin melodies are developed in a song-like fashion. No performer could complain about these works being unplayable.

Beethoven wrote his only violin concerto in 1806. It was dedicated to the young Austrian violinist Franz Clement. The first performance was a disaster. Beethoven failed to complete the concerto in time for adequate rehearsals to take place, and consequently the performer had to read most of the music almost at sight! It was not until long after Beethoven's death that the work became popular in the concert hall.

This impressive picture of Beethoven was painted by the artist Joseph Carl Stieler in about 1819. It shows Beethoven as a handsome and successful composer, although it fails to give any indication of the real man, wracked with the depression that haunted him his entire life.

Left: *Beethoven conducting at the palace of Count Razumovsky in Vienna. The Count was a great patron of the arts, and commissioned three string quartets from Beethoven.*

ON THE CD
Violin Sonata No. 8 in G
Op. 30 No.3 III. Allegro vivace

Beethoven wrote the three sonatas for piano and violin that form Opus 30 in 1802, and dedicated them to Alexander I, Tsar of Russia. The Finale of No. 3 has many brilliant passages for the violin, and is written in rondo form, which means the first tune is repeated many times throughout the movement.

Left: *Beethoven's ear trumpets. Beethoven's worsening hearing did not affect his determination as a composer, although by the age of forty-eight he was almost totally deaf, and conversation with him was impossible.*

This famous caricature of Beethoven by the artist Johann Peter Lyser shows Beethoven walking in his usual way – lost in thought, with his hands behind his back.

SCHUBERT
1797–1828

Franz Schubert loved the sound of stringed instruments playing together, but he especially loved the sound of the violin.

Right: *Central Europeans have always been fond of dancing, whether in a simple rustic setting or at a grand ball. Schubert wrote many sets of dances for use at elegant Viennese parties.*

Op. 94.   Preis: Mark. 1.25.

Verlag und Eigenthum

Schubert's schoolteacher father was a great lover of music and gave his son his first violin lessons. The young pupil made such rapid progress that by the age of nine he had outstripped his father. Under the direction of a new teacher, the parish organist Michael Holzer, Schubert made quite a name for himself in the neighbourhood as a violinist and singer. At choir school he was leader of the orchestra. At home, during the school holidays, the family formed a string quartet, and performed some of the young composer's first works.

Young Franz wrote his first string quartet and a set of German dances for strings when he was only fifteen, and still at school. He worked remarkably quickly at everything he did, and could work equally well in silence or noise. On the manuscript at the end of the first movement of his second quartet he writes, 'written in four and a half hours' – an amazing feat for a sixteen-year-old boy.

Four violin sonatas were all written before his twenty-first year. Like so many of Schubert's compositions, none of the sonatas was published in his lifetime.

Schubert's father, Franz Theodor Schubert, who wanted his son to follow in his own footsteps as a teacher. Although Schubert taught for a while, he hated it. When he finally left teaching to follow a career as a composer it caused much family bitterness.

A Schubert evening by the painter Julius Schmid, with Schubert at the piano. The composer's friends held private concerts of his music which they called 'Schubertiads'. It was at such evenings that many of Schubert's works had their first performance.

ON THE CD
Rondo in A D438

Schubert wrote his Rondo in A for violin and string orchestra in June 1816 when he was only nineteen, although the work was not published until 1897, long after the composer's death. The music begins with a short introduction, leading into the bright rondo theme.

Towards the end of his life Schubert became friends with the Czech violinist Josef Slavík and wrote two works for violin and piano for him – a Fantasy and a Rondo. The Fantasy was performed in public by Josef Slavík the month following its composition; for Schubert to have works performed so quickly after their composition was highly unusual.

Only two or three months before his tragic death in 1828, Schubert wrote his last work for strings: a quintet for two violins, viola and two cellos. Schubert never heard his quintet performed; it lay forgotten, waiting over twenty years for a first performance.

The score of Schubert's popular 'Trout' quintet for strings and piano, written in 1817. The work takes its title from the song of the same name, which Schubert incorporates into the slow movement of the piece.

The house in the Vienna suburb of Neue Wieden where Schubert died, it is thought from typhoid.

SAINT-SAËNS

1835–1921

Camille Saint-Saëns had a long life – composing to the end of his eighty-six years. He was a great lover of melody, and it is his melodic invention that has ensured his compositions are still popular today, almost eighty years after his death.

Musicians, North Africa. Saint-Saëns was a great traveller, and often spent his holidays in Algiers. He would have been very familiar with scenes such as this.

The Conservatoire, Paris, where Saint-Saëns studied from 1848. His skilled musicianship earned him praise from the French composers Gounod and Berlioz.

From an early age Saint-Saëns learnt the piano, and later the organ – he was not a violinist, but he seemed able to write for any instrumental combination. He wrote almost two hundred works in every style and form.

In 1870 Saint-Saëns wrote one of his most popular violin works – Introduction and Rondo Capriccioso for violin and orchestra. In music, the word capriccioso means 'lively and light'; and a rondo is a piece of music in which the most important melody returns many times.

Nearly every composer since Beethoven has written a violin concerto – but very few have written more than one. Saint-Saëns began a violin concerto in 1859, but later abandoned it, reusing the material in his 'Concert Piece' for violin and piano. However, he later wrote three complete violin concertos. He wrote the third concerto for the Spanish violinist, Pablo de Sarasate, one of the most respected violinists of the day, to whom Saint-Saëns had already dedicated his first violin concerto.

Saint-Saëns also wrote chamber music for strings, including violin

sonatas and string quartets. In his well-loved and amusing piece, 'Carnival of the Animals', the violins play a leading part, especially when they represent the raucous braying of the mule.

Above: This photograph of Saint-Saëns dates from about 1907 when he was approaching old age. In his later years Saint-Saëns composed as prolifically as he had done when he was a young man.

Saint-Saëns conducting. The composer enjoyed playing and conducting his own works and was received with great enthusiasm and respect wherever he went as conductor or performer.

ON THE CD
Havanaise Op. 83

Saint-Saëns wrote his popular violin piece, *Havanaise*, in 1887. A havanaise (or 'habanera' in Spanish) is a slow stately dance or song in two time, taking its name from Havana, the capital of Cuba. It has always been a dance particularly popular with Spanish and French composers. Here the solo violin weaves a romantic Spanish melody over the orchestra's rhythmic accompaniment.

TCHAIKOVSKY

1840–1893

Pyotr Il'yich Tchaikovsky was not a violinist, but like many nineteenth-century composers the violin was to him one of the most romantic of all instruments, and he gave it important roles in much of his music.

Russian serfs returning from the fields. The Russians have always been great singers. Tchaikovsky was interested in Russian folk music and often worked it into his compositions.

Tchaikovsky wrote his first important string work – a string quartet – when he was thirty-one. The work was immediately popular because the melody of its slow movement was based on an old Russian folk-song which Tchaikovsky heard a workman singing. When the Russian writer Tolstoy heard this beautiful tune he is said to have been moved to tears.

Tchaikovsky wrote another string quartet in 1874, and the following year composed his first piece for solo violin and orchestra: *Sérénade mélancolique* ('Melancholy Serenade'). In 1877 he wrote a second violin piece, *Valse-scherzo*. This was a much more lively composition, designed to show off the brilliance of the soloist: it is possible that Tchaikovsky was experimenting with writing for the violin before he tackled a bigger work.

Left: The house at Votinsk where Tchaikovsky was born. By the age of five young Pyotr was learning the piano.

Left: *Waltzing at a grand ball in Vienna. Tchaikovsky liked the waltz; his* Serenade for Strings *is just one of the many works in which he incorporates a waltz tune.*

Nadezhda von Meck, Tchaikovsky's generous benefactor, who specified that the composer and she should never meet. Tchaikovsky corresponded regularly with her, telling her about his latest compositions, and often asking her opinion.

The very next year the 'big work' came along: a violin concerto. But Leopold Auer, the violinist to whom the piece was dedicated, refused to play it. He said it was too difficult, and badly written for the instrument! However, he finally agreed to perform the new piece which, although not well received at its first performance, has now become a popular part of the violin repertoire.

It is probably the *Serenade for Strings* that is Tchaikovsky's most well-known piece for strings. He was very pleased with the work, and wrote excitedly to his friend and patron, Nadezhda von Meck, telling her, 'I think the middle movement, played by the violins, would win your sympathy'. In a four-movement work there is of course no middle movement! But Tchaikovsky probably meant the beautiful waltz which forms the second movement, and which has become the most popular and well-known part of the piece.

ON THE CD
Mélodie Op. 42 No. 3

The set of three violin and piano pieces entitled *Souvenir d'un lieu cher* ('Memory of a cherished place') dates from 1878, the same year as the violin concerto. *Mélodie* is the third of the pieces.

DVOŘÁK

1841–1904

As a boy, Dvořák taught himself the violin and performed at village functions. When he was sixteen he began formal music studies which included viola, piano and organ lessons.

When he was twenty-one Dvořák gained a place as a viola player in the orchestra of the National Theatre in Prague. He played in the orchestra, conducted by such great names as Wagner and Smetana, for ten years, while also pursuing a career as a composer.

Like many composers of the nineteenth and twentieth centuries Dvořák wrote only one violin concerto. It was completed in 1879; but when the famous Hungarian violinist, Joseph Joachim, who had recently given the first performance of Brahms's great violin concerto, looked at the work, he found many faults with it. The violinist made suggestions to Dvořák about how the music could be improved. Dvořák accepted what Joachim had said and began further work on the piece. The extra work took the composer almost a year to complete but finally the concerto was given its first performance in Vienna in 1883.

Dvořák moved to America in 1892, where he taught composition for three years. Once, when on holiday in Iowa, he was visited by three Iroquois Indians. Dvořák was very excited when they performed authentic Indian music and dances for him. He incorporated some

From an early age Antonín Dvořák was introduced to the folk-songs and dances of Bohemia. Such music, and similar music of other countries, played a large part in Dvořák's musical output.

Below: *A scene from Dvořák's native Bohemia (now Czechoslovakia).*

Mandan Indian dance. While living in America, Dvořák absorbed the music of native Americans into his own compositions.

Left: Dvořák's family arriving in America in 1892.

ON THE CD
Violin Concerto in A minor Op. 53 III. Finale. Allegro giocoso, ma non troppo

Throughout his life Dvořák was interested in folk music, and incorporated folk tunes into his compositions, or wrote his own melodies in a folk tune style. In the final movement of the violin concerto he uses three folk melodies as his three main themes. The movement is in rondo form.

of the ideas and feelings of their music into his String Quartet No. 6 which he wrote in only three days. As soon as the work was finished it was performed in the village where the Dvořáks were staying, with the composer himself playing first violin. Because the quartet contains many references to native American music it has become known as the 'American' quartet.

As well as composing for violin, Dvořák was interested in teaching it. One of his most talented pupils was Josef Suk. This gifted young violinist eventually became Dvořák's favourite pupil, which is just as well as Suk later married the composer's daughter!

New York at the time of Dvořák's visit was a flourishing musical centre. It boasted two fine orchestras as well as the world-renowned Metropolitan Opera.

GREAT PLAYERS – EARLY

ARCANGELO CORELLI
1653–1713

By the age of seventeen Arcangelo Corelli was already highly respected as a violinist, so much so that he was elected into the prestigious Accademia Filarmonica, the music society in Bologna, Italy, which met to discuss and promote new music.

Corelli is often considered music's first virtuoso violinist – but he was also a fine composer as well as a teacher and orchestral director. Corelli lived most of his life in Rome, rising within a few short years to become the capital's most respected musician.

NICOLÒ PAGANINI
1782–1840

By his early twenties Nicolò Paganini was touring his native Italy impressing audiences everywhere with his virtuoso playing. Tall, slender and wiry, and playing with amazing energy and confidence, many believed him to be inspired by the Devil.

Paganini was also a composer, whose works include chamber music and six violin concertos written for his own concerts. His most famous work is the set of 24 Caprices for solo violin: one of the few pieces he allowed to be published in his lifetime.

After three decades of relentless performing, Paganini's health began to suffer. Tuberculosis plagued his final years, eventually leading to his death.

JOSEPH JOACHIM
1831–1907

Joseph Joachim was born in Hungary and at the age of twelve began lessons with Mendelssohn and Schumann in Leipzig. He was one of the leading violinists of his day and gave the première of Bruch's Violin Concerto No. 1. He was a good friend of Brahms and helped him with his violin concerto, which he later performed.

In 1869 he founded and led the influential Joachim String Quartet. The quartet was particularly admired for its performances of Beethoven and Brahms. Although over the years the other players changed, Joachim always remained leader of the quartet.

GREAT PLAYERS – EARLY

PABLO DE SARASATE
1844–1908

Pablo de Sarasate was born in Spain and gave his first public performance at the age of eight. Later he studied at the Paris Conservatoire, before launching into professional performing life.

He wrote a number of works for violin as display pieces to show off his own skills as a performer. He also transcribed several books of Spanish dances. Many composers dedicated works to him, including Saint-Saëns, Dvořák and Bruch, as well as his fellow violinist, Joachim. Sarasate was particularly known for his beautiful violin tone and smooth, competent technique.

EUGÈNE YSAŸE
1858-1931

The Belgian violinist, composer and conductor Eugène Ysaÿe studied in Brussels with the Polish violinist Henryk Wieniawski and in Paris with the famous Belgian violinist Henry Vieuxtemps. While studying in Paris Ysaÿe formed close links with Fauré, Saint-Saëns, Debussy and other French composers, many of whom later dedicated works to him. From 1887–99 he taught at the Brussels Conservatoire, and in 1894 founded the Ysaÿe Orchestral Concerts in Brussels, which he also conducted.

FRITZ KREISLER
1875–1962

The Austrian violinist Fritz Kreisler entered the Vienna Conservatoire at the age of seven, as the youngest pupil ever, and within three years won the coveted gold medal. At twelve, studying in Paris, he won the prestigious Grand Prix de Rome for his violin playing. At fourteen he toured the United States, and then, still only in his middle teens, he suddenly abandoned music and directed his attention elsewhere.

On his return to the concert platform in 1899 he attracted immediate attention. In 1910 he gave the first performance of the violin concerto Edward Elgar had written for him.

GREAT PLAYERS – MODERN

JASCHA HEIFETZ
1901-1987

Jascha Heifetz was born in Russia and received his first violin lessons from his father. At the age of twelve he toured as a soloist, making his highly successful début in Berlin. In 1917 he left Russia and settled in the USA where he made an immediate impact with his playing. In 1920 he was equally successful in London, performing to an enthralled audience.

Jascha Heifetz also had a successful chamber music career, and transcribed many pieces for solo violin. After a long, worldwide performing life he retired from solo playing in 1971.

DAVID OISTRAKH
1908-1974

The Russian violinist David Oistrakh studied at the Odessa Conservatoire and made his performing début at St Petersburg in 1928. From 1934 he taught at the Moscow Conservatoire.

From the 1950s David Oistrakh established a successful international career with two major débuts – London in 1954 and New York in 1955. In New York he gave the first US performance of Shostakovich's Violin Concerto No. 1, which the composer had written for him. His son Igor, born in 1931, is a noted violinist and often performed with his father.

YEHUDI MENUHIN
born 1916

Yehudi Menuhin was born in the USA of Russian parentage and began playing the violin at the age of four. At the age of seven he made his first public appearance, performing to an amazed audience in San Francisco. By his teens he had established an outstanding international reputation.

In 1932 he recorded Elgar's violin concerto, and was coached by the composer. Late in his career he became interested in Indian music, and performed with the sitarist Ravi Shankar. In 1962 he established The Menuhin School for talented musical children. Since 1959 Yehudi Menuhin has lived in England.

GREAT PLAYERS – MODERN

ISAAC STERN
born 1920

Isaac Stern was born in Russia, later moving with his family to America. He studied at the San Francisco Conservatoire with the violinist Louis Persinger (who also taught Yehudi Menuhin), made his concert début at the age of thirteen, and performed in New York in 1937.

In 1960 he formed a trio with the pianist Eugene Istomin and the cellist Leonard Rose. Isaac Stern has given several important first performances, including *Serenade* by Leonard Bernstein and the Violin Concerto by Peter Maxwell Davies.

KYUNG-WHA CHUNG
born 1948

Kyung-Wha Chung was born in Seoul, Korea. She gave her first public performance at the age of nine, and at twelve began formal studies at New York's Juilliard School, winning the coveted Leventritt Prize jointly with the Israeli violinist Pinchas Zukerman. She made her New York début in 1968 and London début in 1970.

Kyung-Wha Chung is the first Korean musician to win outstanding international success. Other members of her family – her cellist sister Myung-Wha Chung, and pianist brother Myung-Whun Chung – are also extremely gifted.

PINCHAS ZUKERMAN
born 1948

Pinchas Zukerman was born in Tel Aviv, Israel, and studied at the Juilliard School of Music in New York where he won the Leventritt Prize jointly with Kyung-Wha Chung. In 1969 he made both his New York and London débuts, marking the start of a highly successful international career.

He also performs chamber music and has played with the pianist Daniel Barenboim and fellow Israeli Itzhak Perlman. Pinchas Zukerman is also a viola player and conductor.

CD Track Listings

Figures in […] identify the track numbers from the EMI recording
Track lengths are listed in minutes and seconds

EMI is one of the world's leading classical music companies with a rich heritage and reputation for producing great and often definitive recordings performed by the world's greatest artists. As a result of this long and accomplished recording history, EMI has an exceptional catalogue of classical recordings, exceptional in both quality and quantity. It is from this catalogue that EMI have selected the recordings detailed in the track listing below. Many of the recordings featured are available on CD and cassette from EMI.

Antonio Vivaldi 1678–1741
The Four Seasons – Spring
[1] I: Allegro   3.39
Yehudi Menuhin (violin) Camerata Lysy Gstaad
conducted by Alberto Lysy Ⓟ1981

Johann Sebastian Bach 1685–1750
Partita No. 2 in D minor BWV1004
[2] I: Allemande   4.18
[3] II: Courante   2.18
[4] IV: Gigue   3.52
Christian Tetzlaff (violin) Ⓟ1994+

Giuseppe Tartini 1692–1770
Sonata in A minor
[5] V: Allegro assai – Variations 1 to 6   4.48
Stanley Weiner (violin) Jean Lamy (viola da gamba)
Antoine Geoffroy-Dechaume (harpsichord)
Ⓟ1963/DRM 1995#*

Joseph Haydn 1732–1809
String Quartet in D ('The Lark') Op. 64 No. 5
[6] IV: Finale (Vivace)   2.06
Medici String Quartet Ⓟ1977/1995*

Wolfgang Amadeus Mozart 1756–1791
Serenade in G ('Eine kleine Nachtmusik') K525
[7] I: Allegro   5.48
Academy of St Martin-in-the-Fields conducted
by Sir Neville Marriner Ⓟ1977/1986*

Ludwig van Beethoven 1770–1827
Violin Sonata No. 8 in G Op. 30 No. 3
[8] III: Allegro vivace   3.34
Pinchas Zukerman (violin) Daniel Barenboim (piano)
Ⓟ1971/1988*

Franz Schubert 1797–1828
[9] **Rondo in A** D438   13.49
Josef Suk (violin)
Academy of St Martin-in-the-Fields conducted
by Sir Neville Marriner Ⓟ1971/1995*

Camille Saint-Saëns 1835–1921
[10] **Havanaise** Op. 83   9.39
Ulf Hoelscher (violin) New Philharmonia Orchestra
conducted by Pierre Dervaux Ⓟ1977/1993*

Pyotr Il'yich Tchaikovsky 1840–1893
[11] **Mélodie** Op. 42 No. 3   3.30
Ivry Gitlis (violin)   Shigeo Neriki (piano) Ⓟ1985†

Antonín Dvořák 1841–1904
Violin Concerto in A minor Op. 53
[12] III: Finale. Allegro giocoso, ma non troppo   10.07
Frank Peter Zimmermann (violin)
The London Philharmonic conducted by
Franz Welser-Möst Ⓟ1993

                                                                    68.15

                                                            [DDD/*ADD]

Acknowledgements

Macmillan Children's Books would like to thank the following for their permission to use illustrative material reproduced in this book:

a= above, b=below, c=centre, r=right, l=left

AKG, London: 15*a*, 22*l* (Museo Bibliografico, Bologna), 24*a* (Bachhaus, Eisenach), 24*r*, 28*r*, 30*a* (Mozart Museum, Salzburg), 34*r*, 35*a* (Erich Lessing), 36*a*, 39*b*, 40*a*, 41*b*. Bridgeman Art Library: 12*r* (Musée des Gobelins, Paris/Giraudon), 13*a* (Towneley Hall Art Gallery and Museum), 13*b* (Victoria and Albert Museum), 14*l* (Christie's, London), 13*r* (private collection), 23*r* (Philip Mould, Historical Portraits Ltd, London), 27*a* (Agnew & Sons, London), 31*c* (private collection), 33*l* (private collection), 38*al* (private collection), 38*ar* (Christie's, London), 40*r* (Alecto Historical Editions/Joslyn Art Museum), 42*c* (Conservatory of St Peter, Naples/Giraudon). E.T. Archive: 14*b*, 23*a* (Scottish National Portrait Gallery), 26*a* (Castello Sforzesco, Milan), 28*a*, 31*bl* (Mozart Museum, Salzburg), 32*a*, 36*b* (Musée Carnavalet, Paris), 39*a* (Museum der Stadt Wien, Vienna). Fotomas Index: 25*l*, 36*c*. Hulton Deutsch Collection: 44*c*. Lebrecht Collection: 10*c*, 22*bl*, 22*r*, 24*b*, 25*r*, 26*r*, 27*l*, 27*r*, 28*b*, 29*l*, 29*r*, 30*r*, 31*a*, 31*ar*, 32*r*, 33*a*, 33*r*, 34*a*, 34*b*, 35*c*, 35*r*, 37*a*, 37*b*, 38*b*, 40*bl*, 41*al*, 41*ar*, 42*l*, 42*r*, 43*l*, 43*c*, 43*r*. Orbis Publishing Ltd: 8*l*, 9*a*, 9*b*. Performing Arts Library: 6*l* (Jonathan Fisher), 6*r* (Clive Barda), 7*l* (Clive Barda), 7*r* (Clive Barda), 8*a* (Fritz Curzon), 8*r* (Roy Courtnall), 9*r* (Jane Mont), 10*a* (Clive Barda), 10*r* (Clive Barda), 11*a* (Clive Barda), 11*b* (Clive Barda), 11*c* (Clive Barda/Royal Philharmonic Orchestra), 44*r* (Clive Barda), 45*l* (Clive Barda), 45*c* (Clive Barda), 45*r* (Clive Barda). Royal College of Music: 6, 7, 10, 11, 13, 14, 16–21, 42–45 (panels), 48 (background), 5*b*, 23*bl*, 44*l*.

Front cover photograph by Michael Banks (and panel photographs used on pages 1–5, 12, 15, 47.
Back cover: balalaika: Orbis Publishing Ltd; portrait of J.S. Bach: Orbis Publishing Ltd.
Photographs on pages 16–21 by Phil Rudge.
Map on pages 8–9 by Bill Gregory.
Endpapers: score from Beethoven's Concerto No. 5 ('Emperor') reproduced with permission from Eulenberg Editions Ltd.

The publishers are also grateful to:

EMI Records UK for their cooperation and expertise in compiling and producing the CD.

Colin Nicholls (violin maker) for photographs taken at his workshop on pages 16–19, and also the violin featured on the back cover.
Kamera Kids for the model used on pages 20–1.
The Kensington Music Shop for the violin used in the close-ups on pages 20–1.

Every attempt has been made to trace copyright holders.
The publishers would be grateful to hear from any copyright holder not acknowledged here.

Index

all musical works appear in italics